ASTROLOGY FOR KIDS

THE FUN WAY TO LEARN STAR SIGNS, MASTER THE ZODIAC, AND DISCOVER YOUR POTENTIAL FUTURE!

ANIELA PUBLICATIONS

ANIELA
publications

CONTENTS

CHAPTER 1
WELCOME TO THE AMAZING WORLD OF ASTROLOGY!

Thousands of years ago, people believed that the stars in the night sky had special powers. Just like the gods could make changes to your life, everyone thought that the stars could influence people to behave in certain ways. It might sound strange to us now, but back then, it made perfect sense. They already knew that the sun changed the temperature and brought light to the world. They also knew that the moon could control the tides and make the oceans move. So, why wouldn't the stars also control things?

A long time ago, people looking up at the night sky noticed that there were patterns in the stars! They also paid attention and realized that these patterns moved across the night sky, but they always appeared in the same place on the same dates. So these observant people created astrology: an amazing tool to help them navigate the skies and pay attention to what the stars and planets are doing!

Astrologers believe that people on earth can be affected by the position of the stars way up above and that astrology can even tell us about events happening down here on earth. Ancient astrologers separated the year into 12 different pieces, each piece based on a different pattern in the sky. They called these patterns constellations and organized them in a circle they called the zodiac. These 12 pieces are known as Capricorn, Aquarius, Pisces, Aries, Taurus, Gemini, Cancer, Leo, Virgo, Libra, Scorpio, and Sagittarius.

The zodiac shows twelve different signs—sometimes called star signs—and these signs have a strong influence for about 30 days every year. Astrologers believe that each sign can determine what a person will be like if they are born under its influence. They spent years studying the people around them and spotted the similarities in people who were born under the same sign. These traits became the basis for the different star sign personalities.

. . .

Astrology isn't a strict set of personality traits that won't change, but rather a fun way to have a sense of belonging and understanding of things that make us so unique! There are so many things that determine the way we act, feel, or express ourselves. Things like culture, experiences, who our friends are, and so on. So remember, astrology can be a fun way to find out what kind of traits you might share with others that have the same zodiac sign (or even a different sign, for that matter!) You might find yourself saying things like, "I can't help being a bright light in the room; I'm a Leo!" or "Wow! My best friend is so helpful— he's a typical Taurus.

A LOOK INTO THE PAST—WHERE DID ASTROLOGY BEGIN?

Historians think that some form of astrology has been around since we were all living in caves! Cave paintings are simple pieces of art that have been drawn on or carved into the stone walls of caves and mountains. Researchers in charge of studying them have noticed that some of the animals drawn in the paintings are not actually animals at all—they are actually showing the animal constellations in the night sky!

These cave paintings show us that early humans were using the positions of the stars to show the dates of important events like a comet hitting the Earth. Some of these cave paintings are 40,000 years old! Humans have been looking up at the stars for a very long time, and most of them are the same stars that we see today.

THE CONSTELLATIONS

The patterns that people see in the night sky are called constellations. They are groups of stars that can be joined up with an imaginary line to make a picture. Some of these constellations have been found in cave paintings, meaning they are very old. Taurus the Bull was being painted on walls as far back in time as the Bronze Age! (The Bronze Age can be described as the years between 3300 to 1200 B.C., approximately. This is the time when humans invented the wheel and started working with metals!)

Because ancient people could always rely on the constellations being up in the sky, they used them to keep track of time and the months. Just like how you might have a calendar on your cell phone, ancient people used the constellations as a sort of calendar in the sky.

Each star sign in the zodiac is named after a different constellation. Most of them are animals, but others are people or objects that appeared in popular Greek myths.

ASTROLOGY IN ANCIENT CIVILIZATIONS

Cave humans may have been finding patterns in the stars and using them to track dates, but it wasn't until much later that ancient astrologers began to organize this thinking into proper systems. What is really interesting is that people in different countries all over the world were seeing similar pictures and making the same calculations all by themselves.

BABYLONIAN ASTROLOGY

Babylonia was part of Mesopotamia, a large area in the modern-day Middle East. Their astrologers would use the position of the stars and planets to predict the seasons and decide the best time for sowing, harvesting, hunting, and fishing. This was important information for keeping everybody fed and healthy. Babylonian astrologers divided the year into twelve different sections that would later become the signs of the zodiac.

The Babylonians were also big believers in omens. Omens are signs that can tell something good or bad is about to happen. They spotted many of these omens in the stars and would use them to predict big changes.

GREEK ASTROLOGY

The Greeks spent lots of their time invading other countries, and when they did, they would learn about the countries' technology and science. Alexander the Great, an important Greek ruler, invaded Babylonia and brought the secrets of astrology back to Greece. With added information from Greek astrologers, a new form of astrology was born—one that used your star sign to create a horoscope that could make predictions about your life.

EGYPTIAN ASTROLOGY

Astrology in Egypt developed differently from Babylonia. The Egyptians were more interested in recording a regular cycle of stars, so they divided the year into 36 different parts called decans. Each part was signaled by the appearance of a new star. When the Egyptians were invaded by the Greeks, they shared this information with them. The Greeks realized that the decans matched up with their zodiac signs if they grouped them into threes.

· · ·

The Egyptians also linked their decans to the four different natural elements: earth, air, fire, and water. These are still associated with the different star signs today and have become an important part of Western astrology.

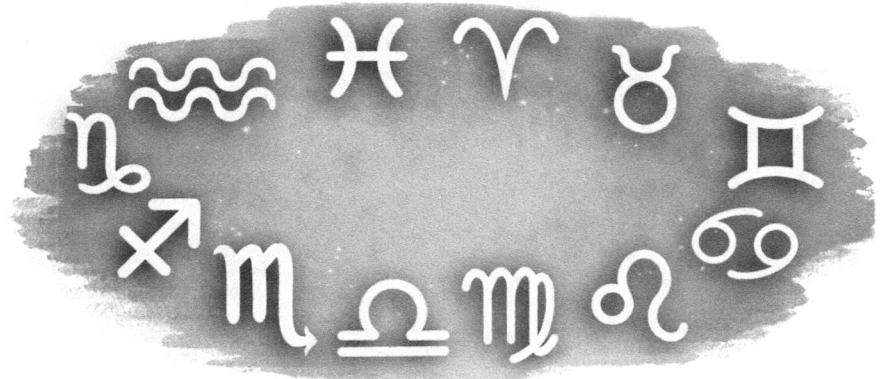

WESTERN ASTROLOGY

All the contributions from these different civilizations eventually led to what we use in astrology today. Western astrology has twelve signs of the zodiac that are arranged in a wheel. This makes it really easy to see the signs that are opposite each other, as well as the signs that are next to each other. Each sign influences the same dates every year, making it really easy to identify your star sign.

Western astrology uses lots of different elements when making a prediction about a person. It looks at their birth sign as well as where the planets were on the day that they were born. This is because Western astrology treats the Earth and everything on it as one single life form, so we are all affected by the same changes that take place.

In Western astrology, each star sign has its own ruling planet. These planets are associated with personality traits and skills that the planet will share with people born under its influence. Each sign is also associated with a natural element. Those signs that share the same element have common likes and behaviors that mean they will get on well with each other.

THE CHINESE ZODIAC

It wasn't just in Europe and the Middle East where astrology was popular; Chinese astrologers had developed their own system at a very similar time. Chinese astrology is different from western astrology because it has one sign for the whole year. Their signs are all named after different animals, but there are still twelve of them. Every twelve years, the cycle repeats itself.

DAILY HOROSCOPE

Dear Gemini, a new and exciting friendship is on the horizon! Be sure to keep your eye out. If someone new in class compliments your shoes, or helps you with a math problem, this could be your new BEST friend!

MAY 21-JUNE20

MODERN ASTROLOGY

Astrology was a really important part of life for people in Europe and Asia for many centuries. Rich people would pay to have their horoscopes read by astrologers and would use this information to make decisions about their life. Even kings and queens would decide battle plans or who to marry based on information from the stars. It was common for royalty to have a court astrologer who was in charge of keeping them updated about lucky times and good omens.

By the end of the 18th century, scientists started spreading the word that there were perhaps more logical explanations for events and that astrology might not be super accurate! This meant that lots of people stopped relying on astrology to tell them things like how the weather would be and where they should build their temples.

Even though some people during this time stopped believing in astrology, there are still countless people today that believe in astrology and use it for lots of different things.

Today, people are far more open to different beliefs, and astrology has returned. We know that science can prove some things, but it cannot disprove others. This means that ancient ideas, including astrology and alternative medicines, have never been proven to be right or wrong. People will make use of these things if they want to. Some people are very serious in their beliefs, while others find astrology to be a resource they can interpret loosely.

· · ·

How you want to use the information in this book is entirely up to you!

CHAPTER 2
FUN STAR SIGN FACTS

Before you go looking up your own star sign, let's have a look at some fun facts about all the different signs. Do you know which star sign has given us the most US Presidents? One fun sign has produced more child actors than any other, and yet another sign is more likely to become a billionaire when they grow up! Maybe this will be a little look into your own future. After all, people often say that your future is written in the stars.

More of the world's top athletes were born with the star sign Aquarius than any other. This includes current sports stars as well as the historical greats from all sorts of different sports. Muhammed Ali, Michael Jordan, and the great Babe Ruth all shared this star sign, so it must be pretty great to be an Aquarius.

.   .   .

Pisces are among the happiest people on the planet, especially at work. They enjoy their jobs more than most of the other signs. Maybe that's because they pick their careers carefully, or maybe they just enjoy feeling useful and being able to make a difference.

Aries are the most careful drivers and follow the rules of the road—so the only tickets they will be getting are from the arcade! But that doesn't mean they're always slow: legendary race car drivers Jacques Villeneuve and Ayrton Senna were born under the Aries sign, and nobody could accuse them of being slow behind the wheel!

Do you find yourself reciting lots of memorized facts and impressing your friends? You could be a Taurus; they are known for having the most amazing memory. Those who are born under the sign of Taurus enjoy retaining huge amounts of information, so they are really good at school tests!

Geminis make natural detectives because they are really observant. They are the sign that is best at solving visual puzzles like spot the difference or word searches. Ok, so word searches aren't going to be the next Olympic sport, but being great at puzzles is a fun party trick to show off with and impress your friends!

Cancers are hard workers and very intelligent, which is why they are one of the signs most likely to be earning more than $100,000 a year! Now, just because you're a Cancer doesn't guarantee you're going to see that kind of money without working super hard, but there's something special about this sign that drives them to do well.

Some of the star signs naturally have a lot of energy, and one of these is Leo. Did you know that you're more likely to find a Leo in the gym than any other sign? They love being active, working out, and staying fit.

Obviously, there are billions of people in the world, so plenty of people share the same birthday. But there's one special birthday that is shared by more people than any other, and it happens to be in the star sign of Virgo. What is that special day? It's September 9th.

. . .

Which star sign belongs to the most billionaires in the world? According to the Forbes Rich List, it's the sign of Libra. There are currently 32 Libra billionaires in the world; that's 12% of the total number of Billionaires! Will you be one of them when you grow up?

Scorpios have also got a lot to live up to because this star sign has given us more world leaders than any other sign: A total of 22 current and former presidents and prime ministers from different countries have been born under this star sign. Even in the US, there have been more Scorpio Presidents than any other sign.

Do you love performing and dream of being on stage or screen? If you're a Sagittarius, you have a good chance of that dream coming true. If you look back at some of the biggest celebrities who stepped into the limelight as a child, around 20% of them —that's a huge amount!—are Sagittarius. This includes celebrities like Britney Spears and Scarlett Johansson.

If you're a Capricorn, you can feel extra special because you belong to the least common sign. This means that there are fewer Capricorns in the whole world than any other zodiac sign. During the dates ruled by Capricorn, you'll also find the two rarest birthdays, which are December 25th and January 1st. It's almost as if parents don't want to have to buy too many gifts at the same time!

Are you ready to find out which star sign is yours? Keep reading, and all will be revealed!

CHAPTER 3
HOW TO FIND OUT YOUR ZODIAC SIGN

You probably know when your birthday is, but did you know that your birthday tells you what your star sign is? When you were born, there was a sign of the zodiac that ruled the night sky. Astrologers believe that the particular sign appearing at the moment you were born would influence your personality throughout your life. Over the next chapters, you'll find out all about the signs of the zodiac and how they can make you brave, caring, fun, and creative. First, though, you need to know which sign belongs to you.

• If your birthday falls on or between January 20th and February 18th, then you are an airy Aquarius.

• From February 19th to March 20th, the ruling sign is Pisces, so if your birthday falls on or between those dates, you're one of these sensitive fish.

• Between March 21st and April 19th, Aries is in charge. This fiery ram sign belongs to you if your birthday falls on or between these dates.

• If you celebrate your birthday on or between April 20th and May 20th, then you are under the influence of the earthy Taurus, the great bull.

• Does your birthday fall on or between May 21st and June 20th? If the answer is yes, then the twins of Gemini will be watching over you with their air influence.

• From June 21st to July 22nd, Cancer the crab is in charge. If your birthday falls on or between these dates, then you'll feel at home with this watery sign.

• Between July 23rd and August 22nd is the domain of Leo, the lion, guiding people born on or between these dates with his fiery roar.

• If your birthday falls on or between August 23rd and September 22nd, you are under the earthy influence of Virgo.

• Are you born on or between September 23rd to October 22nd? If so, you are as balanced as your airy zodiac sign, Libra, the scales.

• From October 23rd to November 21st, it is the time of Scorpio the scorpion. This water sign influences anyone who has a birthday on or between these dates.

• Between November 22nd and December 21st, the sign in charge of the skies is Sagittarius, the archer. If you're born on or between these dates, then his fiery arrows will guide your way.

• Finally, if your birthday is on or between December 22nd and January 19th, you are a Capricorn. This mythical half goat, half fish, is the final earth sign on our list.

Now that you know what your zodiac sign is, you can find out all about what that means. Knowing your sign can help you understand why you like some things more than others. It can also help you to know why you find some things easy and others a bit more difficult.

Don't just read your own sign. Knowing the star signs of your friends and family can help you all understand each other better. Have you got a friend who is always quiet and struggles to keep up with you charging around all the time? It sounds like you're a fire sign, and they're a water sign. Instead of energetic activity, they would love to spend time doing something creative with you. Can you and your best friend spend all day playing in a make-believe world? You're probably both air signs who love to daydream and go on adventures in imaginary worlds.

CHAPTER 4
AQUARIUS

Aquarius comes first in this list because it is the star sign that begins its influence in January, but it is actually the 11th sign of the zodiac. It is an air sign and is often shown by a symbol of two horizontal zigzag lines that are meant to show the wind.

The ruling planet for Aquarius is Uranus, the seventh planet from the sun. This cold, blue planet influences the future, which is why Aquarians are so good at planning ahead. It also lends its color to this cool zodiac sign, making light blue an important influence. Lots of people think that Aquarius is a water sign because it is associated with the color blue, but this isn't the case.

. . . .

Another reason why people wrongly think Aquarius is a water sign is that the constellation of Aquarius, which the star sign is named after, is of a young man carrying a jug of water. This constellation is known as Aquarius, the Water Bearer.

All the signs of the zodiac have their own lucky numbers. They might mean something special to you, or you might get the chance to use them in the future to give yourself some extra luck. For Aquarius, the lucky numbers are 4, 7, 11, 22, and 29.

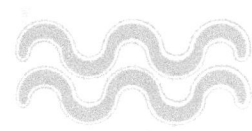

ALL ABOUT THE AWESOME AQUARIUS!

If you are an Aquarius—or you have a friend born under this star sign—you might recognize some of these personality traits. Aquarians like to use their brains a lot. They want to learn new things and have friends that they can talk about them with. This is why they are most happy when working on a group project because they have lots of people to discuss their ideas with.

You can often find an Aquarius deep in thought and trying to solve all the world's problems. However, this does mean that they can get bored quickly if they aren't doing something that challenges them. Aquarians are often drawn to creative subjects like art and music or inventive subjects like science and technology. This is because they can push the boundaries of the subject and come up with new and exciting projects.

Because they like to think a lot, Aquarians are often quiet. You won't often find them charging around and full of physical energy—that kind of behavior is more expected from the fire signs. This quiet quality makes them good listeners, especially if you are telling them your problems. They will be able to help you find solutions and encourage you to think about issues in new ways.

Another good quality that comes from the Aquarius sign is that they want to make everything better. They like to improve the lives of everyone around them. As a grown-up, that could mean creating new inventions or doing charitable work, and as a child, that might mean cutting their neighbor's lawn or helping out with housework. Aquarians like to stand up for what they believe in, which makes them really good at rallying for a cause. An Aquarius would make an awesome class president!

AIRY AQUARIUS ADVENTURES!

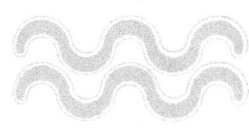

It can take an Aquarius a while to get used to someone, so if you're lucky enough to have one as a friend, make sure you're always kind to them. Aquarius aren't a fan of broken pinky promises or being let down. They take upsets to heart and feel them really deeply. In fact, Aquarians feel all their emotions really strongly, which is great if they're happy and excited about something.

Aquarius people dislike feeling lonely and left out. They love being in a group, but they can also be a little shy about joining in sometimes. The best thing you can do for a friend who is an Aquarius is to invite them to do stuff with you and make sure they always feel included. In return, they'll reward you with interesting conversations, loyalty, and full commitment.

ACQUAINTANCES FOR AQUARIUS!

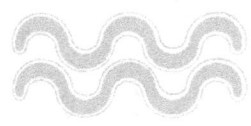

People with the star signs of Libra and Gemini always make good friends with an Aquarius. They are also air signs, and all three tend to think in a similar way. Air signs and fire signs can also make good friends because they can all be quite driven.

Sagittarius also gets on well with Aquarius. The signs are close together on the zodiac wheel, and this means they have a lot in common. Both love to go on adventures and try new things. They also love interesting conversations and activities where they can learn together.

Another good friend for an Aquarius is a Leo. They are opposite signs, but still have a lot in common. They are both loyal to their friends and love spending time in groups. Both these signs care a lot about their friends and will always support them and look after them.

ARTISTIC CAREERS FOR AQUARIUS!

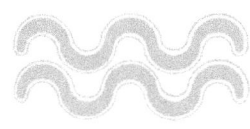

Aquarius signs like to create new things, which is why there are a lot of good Aquarius musicians and actors. If you're feeling shy about standing on the stage, there are plenty of other jobs in the same industry, like making costumes or singing backup vocals in a recording studio.

They're also interested in discovering new things and solving problems, which means that working to develop new technology would keep them fulfilled. Aquarius love to help others, so if that new technology treats diseases or improves society, that's even better. Because Aquarians are so good at explaining things and love to educate others, they often make fantastic teachers.

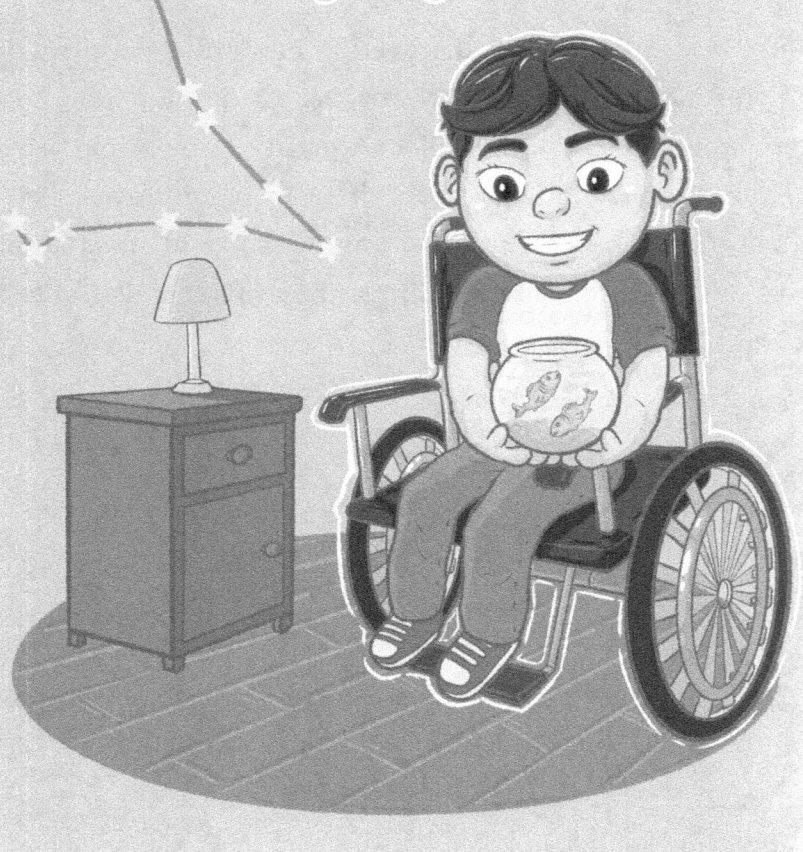

CHAPTER 5
PISCES

Pisces is the 12th and final sign of the zodiac. It takes its name from a constellation of two fish, so it's not surprising that Pisces is a water sign. A special color for Pisces is light green.

Pisces's ruling planet is Neptune, the 8th planet away from the sun. Neptune is called an ice giant because it's big and frosty and covered in icy chemicals, but that doesn't mean Pisces are cold people. In fact, being ruled by Neptune means you have a great imagination and a strong spiritual side.

Like all the other zodiac signs, people born under Pisces have their own set of special numbers that help them in their lives.

You might notice that they keep popping up in things like your phone number, address, or the addresses of your good friends. For a Pisces, the numbers 3, 9, 12, 15, 18, and 24 carry a special meaning.

PRESENTING THE PLEASANT PISCES!

Pisces are big dreamers and will spend their time thinking about mystical and fantastical things. They are extremely open-minded and might get caught up in trying to find answers to the big questions like why is the sky blue, why are flamingos pink, and why do I have to have a bedtime?

If you know a Pisces, they're probably the friend who gives the best emotional support. When you're feeling sad, they'll be there with a shoulder to lean on and an ear to listen to all your problems. Pisces are often called empathetic, which means they are good at sensing other people's emotions and feeling them too. They'll feel happy when you are and sad when you are, which helps to make their friends feel like they're not alone.

Pisces cares a whole lot about their friends' feelings. If you need them, they will make sure to be the best friend they can be and support you. In fact, supporting their friends and family is one of their greatest priorities. If you're a Pisces, then just don't forget to take care of yourself too! But my goodness, aren't your friends and family lucky to have you?

· · ·

Like Aquarius, Pisces love to be creative, and if they're not playing music, writing stories, or painting pictures, they might feel like their energy is getting dull. Lots of Pisces choose one of these hobbies to be a big part of their career, either teaching others or performing themselves.

Pisces are very friendly and enjoy meeting new people, which makes it easy for them to make friends. You know you can trust them with your secrets because they're very trustworthy. A Pisces had a big heart with room in it for everyone. They love their friends, their family, and their pets very much.

PISCES PERSONALTIES ARE SO POSITIVE!

Pisces prefer to see the world in a very positive light, where everyone is friends. So, if they see someone being a big meanie, then this can really upset them. Pisces firmly believe in treating others the way you would want to be treated.

Because Pisces are so creative, they can become sad if someone doesn't immediately enjoy their work. A Pisces will pour their heart and soul into their projects, so if someone doesn't quickly show how much they like it, a Pisces might take this to heart. They create art to make others happy, and when this doesn't work, it can make a Pisces very sad.

PALS FOR PISCES!

Pisces are happy to try and get along with everyone, but they will find that some signs make them happier than others. They are drawn to the other water signs, Scorpio and Cancer, but also find it easy to make friends with the earth signs.

Virgo and Pisces work well together because they both want the same thing from a friendship: someone who is always there for them. Both Virgo and Pisces enjoy helping others and being supportive, so by being friends with a Virgo, a Pisces will also have someone looking out for them.

Taurus is another sign that gets on well with Pisces, even though the two signs have opposite characteristics. A Taurus looks at the world in a very realistic way, and a Pisces is more of a dreamer. Together, they work well to balance each other out. They also both enjoy spending time with someone who can show them different ways of thinking.

PROFESSIONS THAT POWER UP A PISCES!

Because Pisces are so caring, a job where they can look after other people would be very fulfilling. From doctors and nurses to childcare and even pet-sitting, there are many different ways a Pisces can spend their time helping others. Pisces also make good therapists because of their ability to relate to how other people are feeling.

Another good option for Pisces is to do something creative and artistic. They love designing and making something new, telling stories, and adding a little more magic back into the world. An ordinary baker might make cakes, but a Pisces baker will decorate wonderful birthday cakes that will steal the show at any birthday party!

CHAPTER 6
ARIES

When the zodiac was created by ancient astrologers, they chose the start date to be the day in springtime when the sun is right above the Earth's equator. This is called the Vernal Equinox, and it's a special day because the length of the day and the night are exactly the same. The zodiac starts on this day with Aries, the first sign of the zodiac.

Aries is a constellation that looks like a huge ram. In Greek mythology, this ram had a rare, golden fleece. Because Aries is a fire sign, its special color is red. Aries is also ruled by the red planet Mars. Mars is the fourth planet from the sun and is thought to make people determined and driven to succeed.

. . .

People born with the star sign Aries also have their own set of lucky numbers. These are 1, 8, and 17. It's not really surprising that this includes the number one because Aries love to be first at everything!

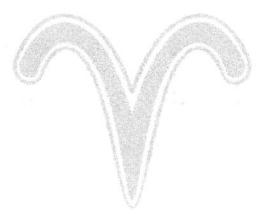

ALL ABOUT THE AMAZING ARIES!

Aries are full of energy. They always have to be doing something, and they can't stand being bored. Whatever they're doing, Aries strive to be the best because they're very competitive. An Aries will work hard and be really focused on learning everything they can do to improve their game. Aries are particularly good at independent sports, such as tennis, golf, and chess because they are so focused. (However, they also make a great team member!)

Do you have something that you love more than anything else and wish everyone else did too? Aries can be really passionate and enthusiastic, and they love sharing this with others. Once an Aries finds what they enjoy, they throw their heart and soul into it.

They are also really determined and don't like to be stuck on a problem. So, if you're an Aries, make sure to take the time to think of the best fix to the problem and not rush in! This can make all the difference.

Aries are really fun to have as friends because they are always thinking of exciting things for everyone to do. They love meeting new people and will talk to anyone without feeling shy or nervous. Aries never worry about what people think of them because they know they're awesome!

It's clear to everyone that Aries is a fire sign because they have so much energy. This fire also powers their emotions, making their inner feelings very obvious. You won't have to guess what kind of mood they're in!

AN ARIES LOVES TO STAY ACTIVE!

Because Aries are so active all the time, it throws them off if there is a delay or an interruption. Because of their fiery nature, Aries don't do well with bore- dom. Although these things might create a grumpy Aries, don't worry, they cheer up super quickly!

Aries can also feel frustrated if they don't think they're showing off their best skill. Aries might feel more at home on the sports field, and they would prefer to use their sporting talent than stay indoors. This is an important thing to think about when picking a career. Aries love to do things they're good at and would rather shine by putting their skills to good use.

ALLIES OF AN ARIES!

The other fire signs, Leo and Sagittarius, will always have a good time with an Aries. These signs are all full of the same bright energy, and they love to be active together. Leo and Sagittarius can keep up with an Aries's thoughts and ideas and will give as good as they get in a discussion.

Leo and Aries are almost always going to be best friends. Both signs love adventures and exploring new things, so when they get together, they will never be bored. Aries and Leo are both really good communicators. They will listen to each other's opinions, even if they are different.

Another sign that gets on well with Aries is Libra. They are on opposite sides of the zodiac wheel, and this means that they have opposite personalities, but that also means that they balance each other. Aries love to lead and make decisions, which is exciting for Libra. Libra people are calmer and more gentle, which means they won't argue with Aries and are more likely to agree with them than disagree.

ADVENTUROUS EMPLOYMENT FOR ARIES!

Aries love a challenge and will often want a career where they can rise to the top. Aries make great salespeople because they find it easy to talk to others. Just like teachers give rewards for good grades and behavior, sales jobs often do something similar for doing well called a bonus, and Aries love striving for a prize!

Aries also make great managers. They love to lead teams and inspire people. Lots of jobs in the business world need managers to run teams of workers, so an Aries can always find a management job in an area that they are interested in.

Because Aries are adventurous, they will enjoy a job that takes them to new places. Working as a tour guide or teaching surfing to tourists would be ideal. Not only can they meet lots of interesting people, but they get to show off their local knowledge. They will also have plenty of free time on their days off to go exploring by themselves or with their friends.

CHAPTER 7
TAURUS

The second sign of the Zodiac is another strong animal: Taurus, the bull. Taurus is an earth sign, and its ruling planet is Venus, the second planet from the sun. This combination makes Taurus want to feel connected to everyone and everything. They are very sensory orientated, which means hugs from their dogs and cats and petting animals are sure to make Taurus happy!

Being an earth sign, it's obvious why Taurus's signature color is green, but they also have another special color: pink. They have special numbers, too, and these can bring a Taurus good fortune. Taurus's special numbers are 2, 6, 9, 12, and 24.

THE TERRIFIC TAURUS!

One of the main qualities of an earth sign is that they are solid and dependable. People who are born under the star sign of Taurus are no different. You can rely on a Taurus to always be there for you when you need them. You can also trust them as a study partner because they will definitely deliver their parts of the project.

Taurus are also hard workers. They won't quit until a project has been completely finished, even if that takes many months. If you need someone to help you finish a long video game, then a Taurus is the one to ask. They don't mind if something takes ages because another good quality of a Taurus is that they are very patient.

You won't often find a Taurus daydreaming away with their head in the clouds. Taurus are very down to earth—what else would you expect from an earth sign?—and although they enjoy the creativity of fantastical worlds and ideas, they often prefer to pay attention to the world around them.

Taurus love to be creative and make beautiful things, especially if this includes natural elements. They are very much at home when gardening and looking after colorful flowers, but they might also enjoy cooking, painting, and playing music. Taurus are very practical, so making things—or looking after things—with their hands will bring them joy.

Although fire signs are super quick to make friends, Taurus, on the other hand, like to take their time. When you're friends with a Taurus, it can be a friendship that lasts a lifetime! Taurus are very supportive friends, and they always offer help: For example, if your bike chain breaks, then they will be the first to help you out.

TAURUS TREASURE TIME AND TASKS!

Taurus are sometimes so grounded in the real world that they can't stand when something changes. A sudden change of plans can upset them and make them feel flustered. Luckily, a good pat on the back and a calm word from their friends are often enough to make them feel stable once again.

Taurus like to think things through carefully and usually have their whole day mapped out. This means they usually like things to go to plan and prefer not to have changes in their day.

TEAM UP WITH A TAURUS!

The other earth signs—Virgo and Capricorn—make good friends for a Taurus. This is because they all think in a similar, practical way. Taurus may find it difficult to get on with the more outgoing signs like Leo and Aries or the imaginative Aquarius, who is always dreaming about the future.

Have you ever heard the saying that opposites attract? It's true for magnets, but it's also true for Taurus and their opposite star sign, Scorpio. Instead of annoying each other with their different ways of thinking and behaving, they are brought together by what they have in common. Taurus and Scorpio are both very loyal and supportive people, which is what you need to build a strong friendship. Scorpio can show Taurus how to be energetic and excited about new adventures, and Taurus will teach Scorpio how to make plans and be reliable.

CHAPTER 1

TREMENDOUS TRADES FOR A TAURUS!

There are lots of things about a Taurus that make them really good workers. Any career that needs them to work on projects, make plans, and think about the small details, will keep a Taurus occupied and fulfilled. Taurus are also fantastic at managing their finances, so working in a bank or in the financial industry would be right up their street.

Working in nature is another great avenue for a Taurus. They would love working as a farmer, looking after animals at the zoo, or studying plants as a botanist. Even a job in a florist shop or as a landscape gardener would be interesting to this earthy sign.

CHAPTER 8
GEMINI

This sign is named after two different people from Greek mythology: the twins Castor and Pollux. This is the third sign of the zodiac and another sign associated with the element of air. Gemini is often represented by the color yellow, making it a bright and cheerful sign.

The ruling planet for all Geminis is Mercury, the closest planet to the sun. Mercury was the messenger for the gods, and this planet makes Geminis really good at communicating with others.

All the zodiac signs have special numbers that are considered extra lucky. Gemini's numbers are 5, 7, 14, and 23. If you're a

Gemini and you notice these numbers appearing in your life, it could be a sign that the universe is sending good things your way.

GLANCE AT THE GREAT GEMINI!

Because Gemini is represented by two twins, they have a whole lot of personalities rolled into one person. Sometimes, a Gemini can seem to switch from one behavior to another—like going from really chatty and friendly to suddenly being quiet and needing to be alone. This is perfectly normal, and part of the fun of knowing a Gemini is that they are so adaptable.

Adaptability makes Gemini the least stubborn of all the star signs. They love change and will often look for new experiences. Gemini rarely stand still and like to hang out with lots of groups of friends, doing different activities and projects. It's a good thing that they make friends so easily because they enjoy a lot of different friends to keep them occupied.

Gemini love to talk, and they are happy chatting away with anyone and everyone. You won't find them starting arguments with people who have a different opinion. In fact, a Gemini is most likely to change their mind if you tell them some new facts.

If you have a Gemini friend, then you are truly blessed because they are the most gentle and kind people. They are also fun-loving and will make sure that you always have a good time together. Geminis care a lot about their friends and will show this by showering them with admiration whenever they get the chance.

GEMINI GLEAM IN GROUPS!

Because Geminis are always on the hunt for something new to do, it drives them bananas to do the same thing over and over. If they get stuck in the same routines, they will try to get out of it any way they can. But of course, everyone needs routines like brushing their teeth and doing homework, so Geminis prefer to make it fun!

Geminis don't like being alone. Even though they love things like reading, listening to music, and watching movies, they would much rather do these things with their friends than by themselves. If a Gemini does decide they need to have some alone time, it won't be for very long, and they will soon be back to their social selves.

GETTING ALONG WITH A GEMINI!

It's almost impossible not to get on with a Gemini because they are so outgoing and friendly. Water signs can find this difficult to handle because they want a deeper friendship, but fire signs love the social energy that Gemini have.

But the best signs to get on with a Gemini are the other air signs, Aquarius and Libra. They love to have long, intelligent discussions and come up with new ideas and adventures together.

Because Gemini have two twins looking over them, they can sometimes feel like two different people. They need a good friend who doesn't mind that they're outgoing one day and want to be home alone the next, and Gemini will find this match in a Sagittarius. Sagittarius are easygoing, and they thrive in changing situations, so they'll have no problem managing a Gemini's colorful emotions. They'll also pull Gemini along on their adventures and introduce them to lots of exciting new experiences.

GREAT JOBS FOR A GIFTED GEMINI!

To be really satisfied in their career, Gemini need to have a job where they do something different every day. They tend to get bored working on the same project until it is finished, and they would much prefer engaging in different activities and being in a different environment as much as possible. This is why Gemini flourish in jobs such as photography or tour managing pop stars, where they will visit a new place and meet new people each day!

Other good careers for Geminis involve situations where they have to communicate well with others, like being a teacher or a tutor. Not only is every day different, but Gemini are so friendly and chatty that they will be able to connect with even the most difficult students.

Geminis love to be their own boss, so working as a freelancer or running their own company is a dream job. When a Gemini is in charge of their own career, they can do exactly what they want and pursue their own interests. When they're inspired by what they love, they will work really hard, so it's a win-win situation.

CHAPTER 9
CANCER

The fourth sign of the zodiac is another water sign. This sign is named after the constellation of a giant crab. You might think that the color associated with Cancer would be red—like a crab —but it's actually white. This makes sense when you find out that Cancer is ruled by the moon.

In fact, Cancer is one of only two zodiac signs that doesn't have a ruling planet. The moon isn't a planet, but it is really important to the Earth because it helps to make the tides flow. This makes it really connected to water, so, of course, it is linked to a water sign.

. . .

Cancer has its own set of special numbers, just like the other zodiac signs. These are 2, 3, 15, and 20. Keep an eye out, and you might see them pop up in your life as good luck charms.

CHARACTERISTICS OF A CANCER!

Emotions are really important to all the water signs. Cancer signs are known to let their emotions make their decisions for them and are usually guided by what they feel. They are often known to make their choices with their heart: if a Cancer wants ice cream for dinner, that's what they're going to have!

Cancers are very good at sensing the emotions of others, and they will do everything they can to make sure that their friends and family feel loved. These people are very special to Cancer, and they can't feel relaxed and at home if anyone they love is unhappy.

Although Cancers enjoy socializing, they really thrive during their "me time." Because Cancers are so independent during their "me time," they find it a lot easier to stay focused without any distractions. This means they are really good at getting their homework done or finishing a project they are working on, such as a painting or coding an awesome video game!

CANCERS ARE CALM AND CARING!

It can take some time for a Cancer to warm up to new people, but when they do, it becomes a genuine friendship. They are sociable but sometimes a little shy. They value a friend they can confide in, so make sure you keep your pinky promises with a Cancer!

Being around family and hanging out at home is really important to a Cancer because this is their favorite space. They have strong family values and will defend their pack like a true hero! You can always rely on a Cancer to stand by you when you need them the most.

COMPANIONS FOR A CANCER!

Because Cancers are so in tune with their feelings, they need friends who understand their quiet nature. The signs most capable of being kind and gentle with Cancer are the other water signs, Pisces and Scorpio. They know what it feels like to be highly aware of your own emotions and can give Cancer the space and understanding they need to feel valued.

Earth signs Capricorn and Libra also get on well with Cancer because they are stable and grounded. They are both loyal and respect the hard work needed to earn Cancer's trust. Capricorn also shares the same work ethic as Cancer—both signs like to focus completely on their projects—so they make a great team. Libra and Cancer both enjoy a super cozy space wherever they are, so Libra knows how important it is to make an awesome environment for Cancer to relax in.

CREATIVE CAREERS FOR A CANCER!

Cancers know how important it is to have a comfortable space, so a career where they help others to find this would be very rewarding. Whether it's working as a realtor, a decorator, or an interior designer, Cancer will thrive in the emotional reward of seeing their customers satisfied.

Architecture is another great career choice that will let Cancers design the homes of others. Architects tend to work by themselves, and their designs can include a lot of fine detail. Both of these things allow a Cancer to be their most productive.

Being able to sense the emotions of others is a strong Cancer trait, and many often seek a career where they can put this to good use. Cancers make great nurses, nannies, social workers, and home carers. They love looking after others and will treat everyone with the same care and respect.

CHAPTER 10
LEO

This outgoing fire sign is the fifth sign of the zodiac. On the zodiac wheel, Leo appears opposite Aquarius, which tells you that these signs have opposite personalities. Leo is named after the constellation of a great lion that prowls the night sky. This sign's colors are bright and fiery: gold, orange, and yellow.

Leo doesn't have a ruling planet; instead, it has a ruling star! Leo is ruled by the sun. The sun is the brightest part of the solar system, and so Leos like to be the most vibrant part of their family and friendship circles, too. They are full of life, and they light up everyone around them!

. . .

Leos should keep an eye out for the following special numbers popping up throughout their life: 1, 3, 10, and 19. If you see one of these, it could be a sign that you're moving in the right direction.

LEARN ABOUT THE LEGENDARY LEO!

The lion is the king of the jungle, and Leos tend to feel like the leader of the pack wherever they go. They love to be center stage and enjoy all that comes with being a star. Leo is never happier than when their talents and personality are on show, whether they're giving a performance or talking in a group.

Leos are great to work with on school projects because they'll take charge and organize everyone. They'll also be more than happy to give the final presentation because they love speaking in front of the class. They get all of their confidence from the ruling sun and can't wait for their chance to shine.

CHAPTER 10

Leos have a kind heart and look after everyone in their pack while making incredible friends. They're always up for fun, energetic, and exciting activities, so you know you will have a good time if there's a Leo in your group.

LEOS LOVE TO LEAD!

Because Leos can come across as very confident, people often forget that they have feelings too. Make sure to treat your Leo friends with the same kindness and compassion that you give to everyone.

Leos are well known for being one of the more willful signs. They know what they want to do and how they want to do it. Getting a Leo to change their mind or to make a compromise takes a lot of negotiating because Leos don't give up easily. This can be a good thing if you've got a problem to solve because Leos will keep working on it until they find the answer!

LINK UP WITH A LEO!

Other fire signs, Aries and Sagittarius, have the same loud and vibrant energy as Leo, so when they all get together, fireworks can happen. This can lead to lots of fun and excitement.

Some signs that make fantastic friends for Leos are the air signs Gemini and Aquarius. Fire needs air to burn, so it totally makes sense that fire and air signs make great friends. The air signs like a challenge, and trying to energetically keep up with a Leo is certainly that.

LIVINGS FOR A LEO!

Leos are great in the limelight, so any career where they can take a starring role is perfect. Being an actor or a politician will bring Leo lots of adoring fans. For those Leos who prefer to be a little more in the background but still want to enjoy the rich and famous lifestyle, there are plenty of careers, such as being a talent agent, personal assistant, or photographer.

Being creative comes naturally to Leos, so they will also enjoy a job where they get to use their arty natures. Being an artist or a designer could be fun for a Leo. They're also not afraid of hard work, so they will happily put in the effort needed to market their work and make a name for themselves.

CHAPTER 11
VIRGO

Virgo is the fifth sign of the zodiac and comes at the time when summer is turning into fall. As an earth sign, Virgos feel very connected to nature and the changes that are happening. Even the constellation Virgo shows the goddess of the harvest holding a stalk of wheat.

Virgo follows Leo, and they have similar special colors, but Virgo's colors are more muted. They are pale yellow, beige, and gray. Virgo's ruling planet is Mercury—the same planet as Gemini. This helps Virgos to communicate well with others.

All the star signs have some numbers that can be lucky for them. These numbers might appear in your life, or you could choose them on a sports jersey or locker combination. The lucky numbers for Virgo are 5, 14, 15, 23, and 32.

VITAL FACTS ABOUT THE VIBRANT VIRGO!

Virgos are absolute perfectionists. Everything they do, right down to the tiniest detail, has to be the best. At school, Virgos make sure that their projects are packed full of great information. They always work hard and enjoy practical tasks like building models and doing science experiments.

They pay the same attention to their friendships. They always remember everyone's birthday, what their favorite snack food is, and who likes what sports. They work hard to make sure that everyone else is enjoying themselves, but this can mean that they don't get a lot of time to do what they want. Virgos aren't good at just doing nothing either, so they find it difficult to relax.

VIRGO

Virgos can be a little hard on themselves when they think they haven't done something to the best of their ability. They need to have good friends around them to remind them of how awesome they are!

VIRGO'S VALUES!

Unlike the chatty fire and air signs, Virgos can be shy around groups of people they don't know well. They would much rather spend time with a small group of good friends than go to a big, loud party.

Virgos are gentle, loving, and caring, and they prefer to be around others that feel the same way. They really don't appreciate it when someone isn't kind, no matter what the circumstances.

VISITORS FOR VIRGO!

Virgos feel most at home when spending time with other earth signs. They share their down-to-earth way of thinking and their love of nature. Virgos also have good friendships with the water signs Cancer and Pisces.

Pisces are happy to let Virgo take their time making friends because they know this will lead to a deep friendship. Cancer and Virgo both have a similar approach to work—they like to get all the details right—so Cancer will understand Virgo's need to take care in everything they do.

VOCATIONS FOR A VIRGO!

Being detail-oriented makes Virgo ideal for careers in science and mathematics. Accountants work with other people's finances and make sure there are no errors in their paperwork—something that a Virgo would love. There are a lot of fine details to be worked on as a researcher, and Virgos make very careful scientists.

Virgos are good communicators, so they would also enjoy working as an editor. It would be their job to make sure that there were no mistakes in books before they were published. They have great attention to detail and wouldn't get bored, even if it took them days to read everything through. They would also enjoy helping to send stories out into the world.

LIBRA

CHAPTER 12
LIBRA

This air sign is the seventh sign of the zodiac. Libra is named after the constellation, which is a picture of a set of scales. This helps Libras to be balanced, and they don't like it when people go to extremes. Libra is ruled by Venus, which also means they are all about finding harmony.

The colors most associated with Libra are pink and green. These colors might not seem like they go well together, but this suits the part of Libra's personality that wants to make peace between different sides.

Libra has a set of special numbers, just like all the other signs of the zodiac. These are 4, 6, 13, 15, and 24. If you are a Libra, keep an eye out to see if these numbers appear in your life. If they do, they might mean you are in for some good luck!

LEARN ABOUT THE LOYAL LIBRA!

Libras often feel like it's their duty to solve all the world's problems, and they don't like anything that isn't fair. Libras are very good at deciding how to share things equally and finding solutions to problems that suit everyone. If you're working in a group, you can rely on the Libras to make sure that each person does their fair share of the work and gets equal praise at the end.

Like other air signs, Libras don't like to fight. They are very peaceful people and stay out of arguments as much as possible. However, it's not possible to make everyone happy at the same time, even though Libras always try their very best. They like talking to others and are at ease in groups of people.

As you would expect from a sign that doesn't like conflict, Libras are very gentle and caring. They will go out of their way to make sure that they never upset their friends. Libras are great at talking through their problems and letting everyone know how they are feeling, and they can also inspire others to do the same. Once they've got everybody talking, they can use their diplomatic skills to settle any problems.

Because Libras don't like to say or do anything that will upset anyone, they will often wait to see what others will say or do before offering their own opinion. This is extremely considerate. However, if you're a Libra, don't forget that your opinion matters too, and sometimes it's worth speaking up!

LIBRAS WILL LIFT YOUR SPIRIT AND LISTEN!

Libras are all about balance, so they can't stand to see any injustice and will jump in to help whenever possible. They get really upset if they see things like bullying or inequality. This could be in their own friendship group, in school, or in the wider world. When a Libra spots something out of harmony, they will do whatever they can to make things right, even if they didn't cause the problem.

Libras can't stand mess! They really appreciate and take care of their things, like clothing, technology, toys, and furniture. This is great news for parents, as a Libra will keep their room tidy without having to be told twice!

LIFE LONG FRIENDS FOR LIBRA!

The air signs—Aquarius, Gemini, and, of course, other Libras—will understand Libra the best, and these make for life-long friends. They will respect Libra's commitment to justice and not pull them into arguments for fun.

Surprisingly, Libra can get on very well with Aries and Sagittarius, despite them being fire signs. They understand Libra's passion for harmony. Aries is the opposite sign to Libra, meaning they're on different sides of the zodiac wheel. Opposites can work really well together as friends because they balance out each other's behaviors. Libra can calm down Aries and help them to see the other side in a disagreement. Aries can inspire Libra to become more self-assured and stand up for themselves!

LINES OF WORK FOR A LIBRA!

Because Libras are committed to fighting injustice and restoring harmony, they like to choose careers where they can make a real difference. Working as a lawyer is an obvious choice, but if that doesn't sound like fun, there are other jobs working with the law that will also satisfy a Libra. Legal secretary, clerk, and judge might also appeal to Libra's sense of justice.

Because of a Libra's goal of restoring harmony on the planet, they may pick a career that will help the environment, such as an environmental or conservation scientist!

A counselor or psychiatrist is another good choice. Both jobs involve helping others to talk through their problems, and this means Libra can use their excellent communication skills. Whether they're helping people to solve an inner conflict or a disagreement with another person, Libra will feel happy knowing that they have helped to bring a little more harmony into the world.

CHAPTER 13
SCORPIO

Scorpio is the eighth sign of the zodiac, and it belongs to the group of star signs called the water signs. This is strange because scorpions—the animal that Scorpio is named after—live in the desert, where there is very little water. Scorpio's influential colors reflect this because they're not watery colors at all: they are scarlet, red, and rusty orange.

The ruling planet for Scorpio is the planet Pluto—even though it is no longer called a planet by NASA, it can still have an influence on our lives. Pluto is all about change and transformation, and Scorpios often have multiple layers to their feelings and their personality.

. . .

There are some special numbers that Scorpios might like to keep in mind. These numbers can be lucky for you or might help you make the right choice if they pop up in certain situations. These special numbers are 8, 11, 18, and 22.

SAY HELLO TO THE SENSATIONAL SCORPIO!

Like the other water signs, a Scorpio is very in tune with their emotions. It might not seem like they are, though, because they are very good at looking calm on the surface when they might actually be a little bit upset. Being able to stay calm, even when everything is going wrong, is something that makes Scorpios natural leaders!

Scorpios love to be successful in everything that they do. Once they know what they want, they are really focused on getting it. They're great to work with because you know that they won't avoid their responsibilities. It's not just hard work that makes Scorpios successful: They're very charismatic, fun, and incredible at making friends!

Just like the scorpion, Scorpios aren't afraid to take on big challenges. They are very brave and will always stand up for what they believe in. You can count on Scorpios to make positive changes in the world!

SCORPIO'S ARE STAND UP SIGNS!

Once a Scorpio trusts you, they'll open up and share a whole new side that you didn't know they had. Being trusted by a Scorpio is a true privilege, so make sure they can count on you.

Standing up for their beliefs is a core Scorpio trait, and when they believe they are right about something, they will stick by it! However, if you offer a different perspective, then a Scorpio will always hear you out.

SIDEKICKS FOR SCORPIO!

Scorpios get along the best with water signs because they understand their emotional qualities the best. Cancer is especially good with Scorpio because they can sense their hidden emotions and know just what to say to calm them down and help them settle.

Another sign that gets on well with Scorpio is Taurus. This grounded earth sign isn't easily flustered by Scorpio, and in return, Scorpio appreciates the reliability and predictability of a Taurus friend.

SUCCESSFUL PROFESSIONS FOR SCORPIO!

Scorpios will work hard at whatever task they are given, but they really like projects that they can dedicate their time to. They love digging into the finer details, so a job as a researcher is ideal. Working alone suits a Scorpio, and they will enjoy showing others their findings and sharing their incredible knowledge on a subject.

Another good job would be working as an engineer. This career allows Scorpio to spend all day fixing problems. They will also enjoy seeing the real-world benefits of their work, and engineering projects often result in a new machine, building, or infrastructure.

Any career path that gives a Scorpio a chance to challenge themselves is going to appeal to them. They enjoy success and being the best that they can be, no matter how much hard work it takes. Something like a detective or a surgeon, where their commitment and their strengths will be recognized, would be an ideal choice.

CHAPTER 14
SAGITTARIUS

This energetic fire sign is the ninth sign of the zodiac and is ruled by the king of the planets, Jupiter, the fifth planet from the sun. This planet is all about positive vibes, bringing luck, hope, prosperity, and growth to those under its influence. Sagittarius influences some of the darkest months of the year, and to make up for the lack of light, this star sign creates some of the most bright and uplifting people.

Despite being a fire sign, the influential color for Sagittarius is blue. This might be a link to their traditional role as a healer: Sagittarius's constellation is the centaur Chiron, who was a great teacher and healer in Greek mythology.

. . .

Sagittarius has a set of special numbers that can have a strong influence on the lives of people born under this sign. These numbers are 3, 7, 9, 12, and 21. If you're a Sagittarius, you might notice these numbers appearing in your life to show you that you're on the right path.

STARRING THE SINCERE SAGITTARIUS!

Following the intense Scorpio, Sagittarius is the exact opposite. People born under this sign are eternal optimists, always seeing the best in people and situations. They expect everyone to be as good and kind as they are and are always open and honest about these expectations.

Sagittarius love people. They always want to find out new things about different cultures and different places, and the best way to do this is to talk to people who have lived there. A Sagittarius's friendship group will be large and filled with all sorts of different people rather than just those who are like them. They are more than happy to spend time with people they have nothing in common with: Sagittarius sees this as an opportunity to try something new rather than writing off a friendship straight away.

Because Sagittarius is always trying to learn or do something new, they can get frustrated when stuck in the same routine. They love to learn new things and are really good at researching and teaching themselves. You might also find that they offer interesting new perspectives that you hadn't thought of before.

SAGITTARIUS'S ARE SELF-SUFFICIENT!

Sagittarius love to be free to follow their own path and set their own boundaries; they really do march to the beat of their own drum. They take their friends on the best adventures, often taking them places that they've never been!

Part of being such an open and honest sign is that Sagittarius people are never afraid to say what they mean. They don't get upset too easily, but of course, they would like to have their opinions valued and not overlooked. Even if a Sagittarius accidentally said something that upset someone else, then they likely didn't mean it to come off that way because they are loving and helpful.

SOCIALIZING WITH A SAGITTARIUS!

Aries makes an excellent friend for Sagittarius because they have many things in common. Both are fire signs, meaning that they are full of energy and love doing exciting and adventurous things. They both love to try new activities, so visiting a new trampoline park in town or eating at a new pizza place would be the perfect time for this adventurous duo!

Gemini also get on well with Sagittarius. They don't like being still and can't wait to try new things. Together, Gemini and Sagittarius will push each other to find new hobbies and activities that will keep them from ever getting bored.

Sagittarius might not quickly relate to the water and earth signs and their attachment to their homes. Why stay still when there is the whole world waiting to be explored? If you know someone who finds it hard to sit still and always seems to be trying something new, it's very likely they're a Sagittarius!

SUPERIOR WORK PLACES FOR SAGITTARIUS!

Sagittarius are fun-loving adventure seekers and would be happy in any job that lets them indulge this side of their personality. The travel and hospitality industry is a great starting point. Sagittarius would love working as a travel agent, where they can help others to design their perfect holiday. This will also give them the insider track on some great travel deals for their own vacations!

The creative side of a Sagittarius can be a huge asset at work, and a career as a freelance artist, designer, or architect could be just what they need to showcase their unique style. Bold and adventurous designs won't scare a Sagittarius, and they will enjoy the freedom of working on their own projects as their own boss.

A repetitive 9-5 job will likely stifle the Sagittarius's enthusiasm, so they might prefer to find a job that has some variety. Being a teacher fits the bill perfectly. Every day is always different, and Sagittarius will get to use their excellent communication skills to inspire the children in their class.

CHAPTER 15
CAPRICORN

Capricorn is the tenth sign of the zodiac and the one that starts the latest in the year: on December 22nd. This sign is represented by the constellation Capricorn the Sea Goat—a mythical creature that has the head and hooves of a goat but the tail of a fish, a bit like a mermaid!

Despite living in the sea, Capricorn is an earth sign. To show this, the sign is associated with neutral, earthy colors, including brown and black. The ruling planet for Capricorn is Saturn, the largest planet in our solar system and the sixth planet from the sun. Saturn is the planet of responsibility, strength, and discipline: All qualities that you will find in a Capricorn.

. . .

CHAPTER 15

Just like all the other star signs, Capricorn has their own set of lucky numbers. These are 4, 8, 13, and 22. These numbers can help you in your life by guiding you to make the right decisions, so watch out for them.

CELEBRATE THE COOL CAPRICORN!

Capricorns are the opposite of their zodiac neighbors Sagittarius. They love structure and having everything set out in order. If you give a Capricorn clear instructions, they will follow them absolutely, making them excellent study buddies and work partners. They are also very disciplined and can stay focused on the same task for a long time.

Being an earth sign means that Capricorns are very grounded in reality. They often prefer quieter hobbies like reading rather than active hobbies like sports but not always.

Capricorns give their friends the same focus they would give to their work, which makes them excellent pals. Their reliability is one of their best qualities, so they will be sure not to miss a birthday, soccer game, or anything that means a lot to you.

CAPRICORNS CHERISH TRADITIONS!

Capricorns really value their boundaries and don't like to change the familiar ways they do things. They often worry that change won't be good, so it's really important to remind your Capricorn friends (or yourself) that change can be really cool! Imagine a world where you didn't discover your favorite cereal or cartoon because you didn't want to try something new!

Because Capricorns aren't a fan of change, traditions mean a lot to them. This makes them very close to their families, and they really enjoy reliving the memories that traditions bring. They love to remember things like seasonal holidays and family vacations and will be the ones taking lots of photos! So, something like the pizza place their family takes them to every birthday means the world to them, and they look forward to these things every year.

COMRADES FOR CAPRICORN!

Capricorns get on well with all the earth signs, but especially with Taurus. They share a mutual love of being practical and are both hard workers. Taurus lives in the present while Capricorn lives in the past, but these two views work well together, with Taurus encouraging Capricorn to appreciate today.

The air signs—who are always planning for the future—and the fire signs—who are always in search of fun—might find it difficult to be on the same calm level as a Capricorn. Although they might make interesting friends, Capricorns usually prefer to engage in more familiar and peaceful activities at home. One sign that shares a similar enjoyment of home comforts is the water sign, Cancer. Capricorn and Cancer will enjoy a relaxed friendship where they can stay in with a good movie and some popcorn.

CAREERS FOR A COMMITTED CAPRICORN!

Capricorns love to work and can often find it difficult to stop! Finding the balance between their studies or their career, and their friends and family is difficult for this dedicated and driven earth sign. They also want a career with a clear role where they know exactly what is expected of them.

A high school teacher would be the perfect job for a hard-working Capricorn. They love the planning and organization involved and are patient enough to deal with the difficult behavior of some teenagers. The long school holidays also force Capricorn to take a much-needed break and enjoy some relaxing hobbies and hanging out with friends.

Another career that is well-suited to Capricorns is that of a realtor. Hard work is vital in this business if you want to be a success, and Capricorns definitely have enough drive and determination to be great! There's also the chance to manage your own workload, and most realtors work alone or in small teams, which suits a Capricorn completely.

A ZODIAC STONE FOR EACH STAR SIGN!

Did you know that each astrological sign has a special mineral or gemstone that is linked with it? Most people know about birthstones, but zodiac stones are a little more specific. Some people like to wear these precious gems to bring good luck, and others just like to keep them around as decoration or in a special box or pouch. Want to know your zodiac stone?

A ZODIAC STONE FOR AQUARIUS: AMETHYST

Amethyst comes in varying shades of purple and violet. One of the countries that produces the most amethyst is Brazil. If you treat amethyst with heat (this means heating it up), it can actually resemble a stone called Citrine. Some people find this stone helps promote calmness and creates clarity in making decisions.

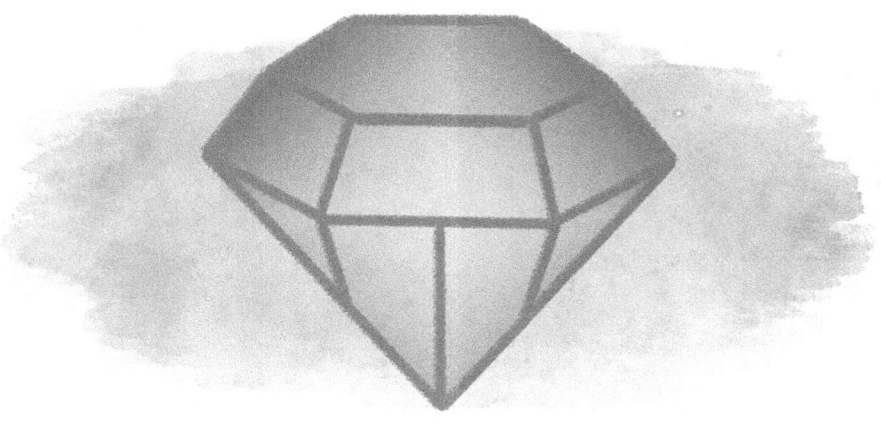

A ZODIAC STONE FOR PISCES: AQUAMARINE

This stone gets its name from the Latin words "Aqua" and "Marina," which translates to "Water" and "Of the Sea." It's no wonder why they named this stone after water and the sea; its colors range from shades of blues and greens that blend together. Some people find this stone empowering and helpful with clear communication!

A ZODIAC STONE FOR ARIES: DIAMOND

Diamonds are made of pure carbon, meaning they are the only gem on the planet made of just one element! Although the most common diamond is translucent (clear), they come in a variety of colors like yellow, pink, blue, and many more. The diamond is one of the four main precious stones on earth. Some people believe this stone promotes powerful inner strength.

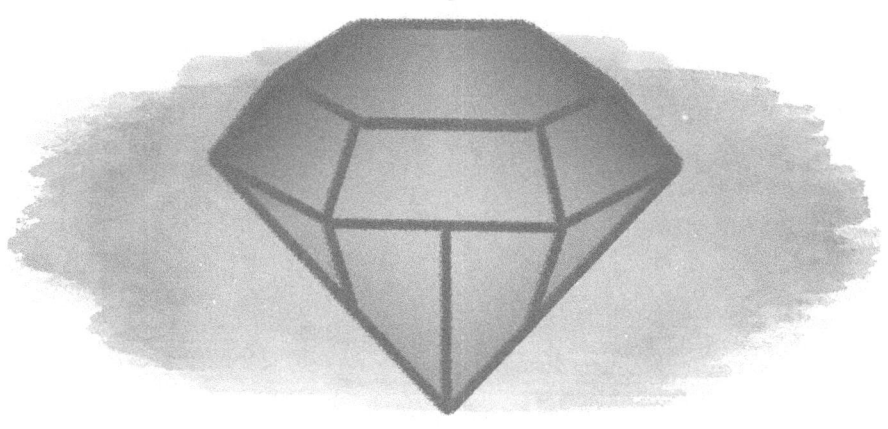

A ZODIAC STONE FOR TAURUS: EMERALD

The emerald is one of the oldest and most sought out stones in history; In fact, it was Queen Cleopatra's (Queen of ancient Egypt) favorite! Its color is a deep vibrant green. The emerald is one of the four main precious stones on earth. Some people believe this stone promotes prosperity (well-being), wealth, and a sense of peace.

A ZODIAC STONE FOR GEMINI: AGATE

There are so many types of agate, from blue lace agate (blue), moss agate (green), and fire agate (red). These stones vary in color but share a resemblance because of the unique banding (stripes). These stones are a type of quartz called Chalcedony. Some people believe this stone promotes inner stability and raises consciousness.

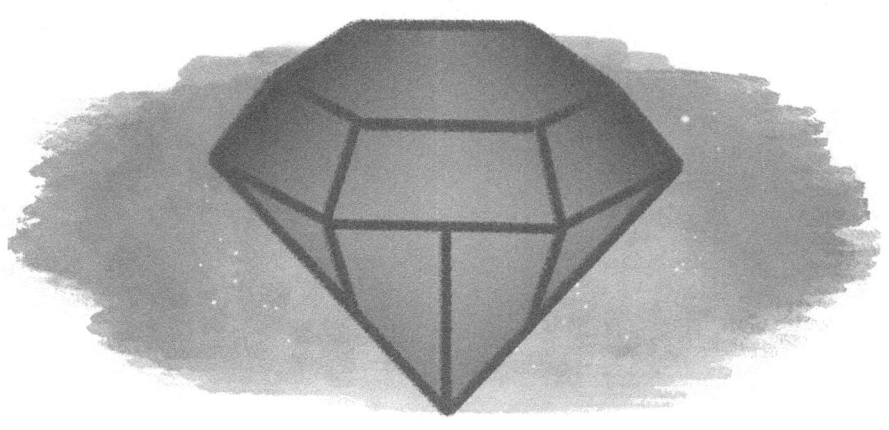

A ZODIAC STONE FOR CANCER: RUBY

The ruby gets its name from the Latin word "rubens," which translates to "red." They are mostly known for being red but can also come in a shade of pink. The ruby is one of the four main precious stones on earth. Some people believe this stone promotes confidence and balance.

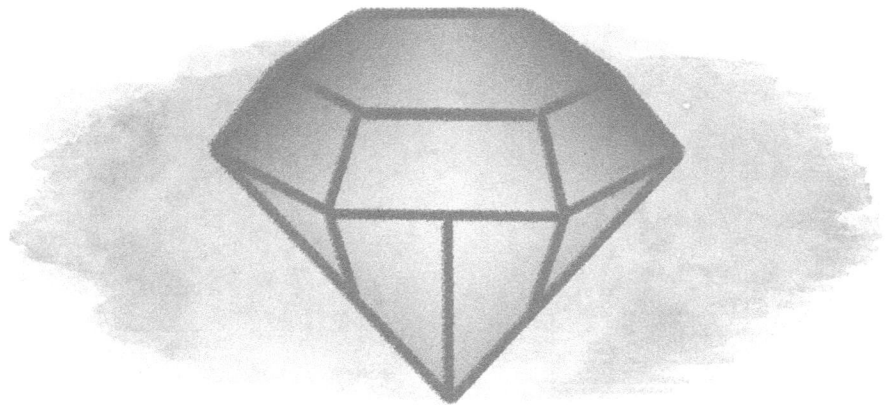

A ZODIAC STONE FOR LEO: PERIDOT

Peridot is one of the only stones that comes in one color, which is green. It is also one of the few stones to be reported outside of earth and found in some meteorites! Some people believe this stone promotes compassion and good fortune!

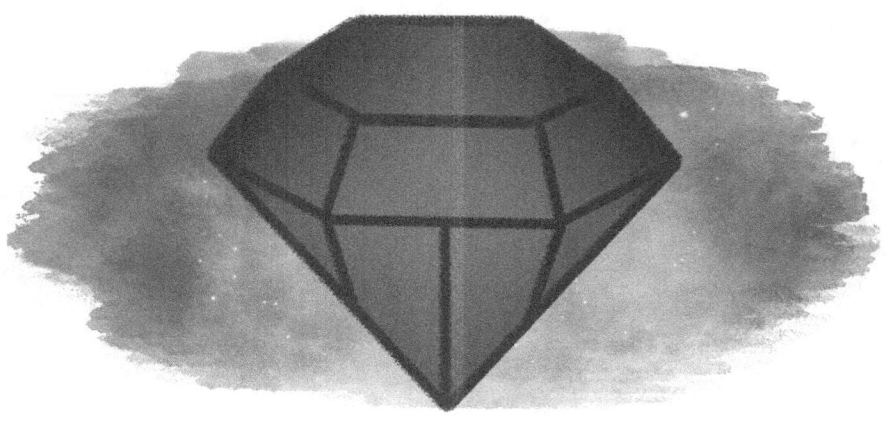

A ZODIAC STONE FOR VIRGO: BLUE SAPPHIRE

Sapphire's color is a deep vibrant blue. Sapphire's name derives from the Greek word "sappheiros," which translates to "blue Stone." The sapphire is one of the four main precious stones on earth. Some people believe this stone promotes self-expression and empathy!

A ZODIAC STONE FOR LIBRA: OPAL

Opal's name derives from the Latin word "opalus," which translates to "precious stone." It is said that about 95% of opal comes from Australia. The color of opal can be described as a milky white or translucent color with shimmer speckles of the rainbow. Some people believe this stone promotes harmony and hope!

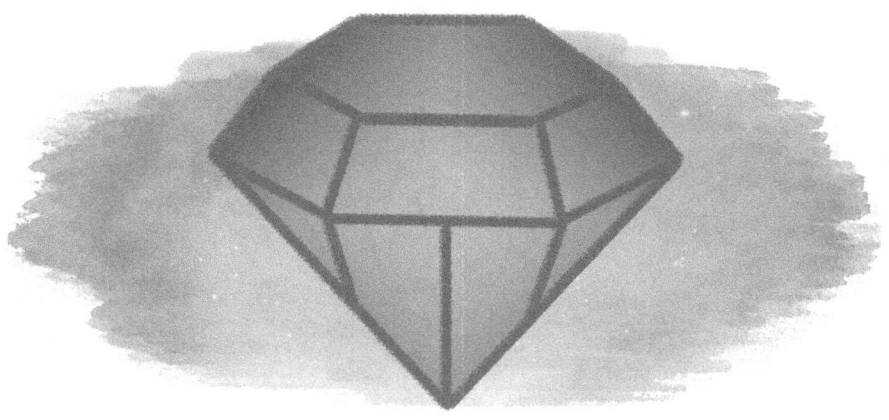

A ZODIAC STONE FOR SCORPIO: TOPAZ

A pure topaz is colorless, so it can often be mistaken for a diamond. They come in many shades of the rainbow, like red, blue, pink, yellow, and green! Red being the most rare, and blue being the most common. Some people believe this stone promotes joy and enthusiasm!

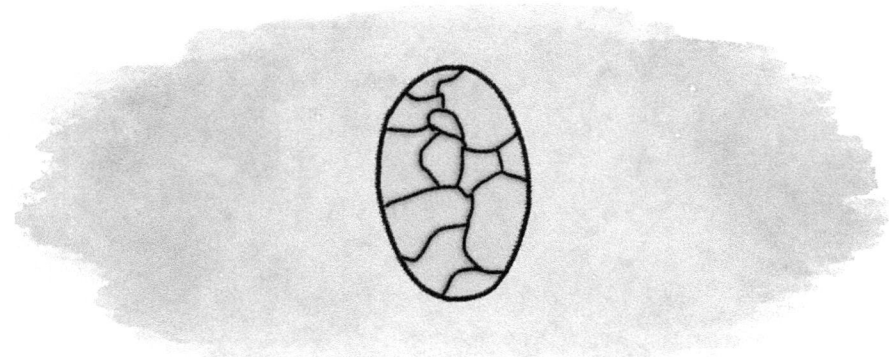

A ZODIAC STONE FOR SAGITTARIUS: TURQUOISE

Turquoise is the only gemstone in the world to have a color named after it. Turquoise's name derives from the French word "turquoise," which translates to "Turkish." Some people find this stone promotes good luck and protection!

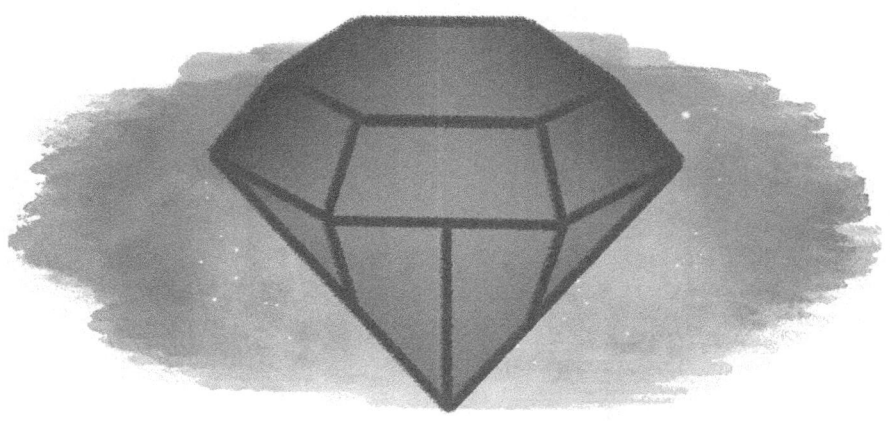

A ZODIAC STONE FOR CAPRICORN: GARNET

Garnet's name comes from the Greek word "granatum," which translates to seed or grain because it resembles the shape and color of a pomegranate seed. Most of the time, garnet is described as a red color, but it actually comes in many different colors, such as green, pink, or gold! Some people find this stone helps promote confidence and boosts their self-esteem!

CONCLUSION!

CONCLUSION!

Have you found it interesting learning about the star signs? I bet you know a lot more now than you did at the start. You're now one of the millions of people, all through the ages, who have started to unlock the secrets of the stars. Next time someone asks you what your star sign is, you can give them a confident answer!

Now that you know all about your star sign, you might understand yourself a lot better. Are you a workaholic Capricorn or a daydreaming Aquarius? Maybe you're a fun-loving Leo or a Cancer who loves curling up at home. Knowing your star sign can help you to see how unique you and your friends are. If they love to speak to everyone, but you feel a little shyer than them, it could be because of the stars above!

What's exciting is that everything you've just learned is only the beginning. There's a lot more to astrology than will fit into one book. If you are interested in investigating further, there are lots more things you can learn.

One thing people love about knowing their star signs is that they can read their horoscope. A horoscope is a prediction of what is going to happen. You can get them for the day or for the whole year. They're often very general and are up to you to work out how they apply to your life, but it can be fun to read that you're going to have a great day!

CONCLUSION!

Not everyone you meet will believe in astrology, and that's ok. Nothing about astrology is a fact; rather, it's supposed to be a guide. Not everything about your sign will fit exactly with who you are, but some parts might be very accurate. Whether you want to use astrology as a bit of fun or you want to look into it in more detail is up to you. It's always good to learn something new, and now you know all about how astrology started and what the different star signs mean!

Have fun on your astrology adventure! Thank you for reading!

YOUR FEEDBACK IS VALUED!

Hey! I just read your daily horoscope, and it said something amazing!

What's that?

It says that your star sign is so kind and always helps others. It also says today is a great day to do so!

Did you know that you can help us by leaving a review for this book on Amazon or Audible?

Ok, good to know that we can help!

Thank you, we can't wait to see you in the next book!

As an independent publishing team floating through space, it would mean the UNIVERSE to get your feedback. It will help us create better books for you and help educate other curious minds even more!

Aniela Publications

www.ingramcontent.com/pod-product-compliance
Lightning Source LLC
Chambersburg PA
CBHW071408120626
46546CB00002B/857